Courage in my Carry-On

———————

Courage in my Carry-On

Rachel Hamilton

ZA
ZealAus Publishing

Courage in my Carry-On

Copyright © 2020 by Rachel Hamilton
Illustrations © 2020 by Rachel Hamilton

www.zealauspublishing.com

All rights reserved. No part of this book may be reproduced or transmitted in any form or by any means without written permission of the author. Some names have been changed to protect the identity of persons.

ISBN: 978-1-925888-68-3 (e)

ISBN: 978-1-925888-69-0 (hc)

ISBN: 978-1-925888-70-6 (sc)

Dedicated

to Mum and Dad.

You are my inspirations and everything

I hope to one day be.

———————

Contents

Introduction	1
Growing Up	2
Sri Lanka	10
India	29
Home from Sea	31
Nightmare	33
Sickness	37
Cambodia	44
Thailand	55
Uganda	63
Back to Uganda	83
Heroes	96
Your Story	99
Thanks	104
About the Author	107

Rachel Hamilton

Introduction

Ever been scared? Afraid of what people think of you? Insecure?

You want to be seen and heard, but you feel invisible?

I get it. See, I've never been very good speaking up. When I was little if someone tried to interact with me, I would start crying, I stopped that as I grew older (thank goodness) but I'm still not good at expressing myself. I've always been afraid of saying or doing the wrong thing.

Stand up and be heard? No thanks, I wanted to blend into the wallpaper.

But at nineteen I took a chance on being brave.

This is my story.

Ten years on, I daily aim to live a life beyond the fences of fear. Fear of failure, judgement, hurt, and the unknown. Sometimes freedom is just beyond that one courageous step.

Growing Up

I grew up in the North Island of New Zealand. I was the second of four children and I loved my little brothers. From the age of four, I wanted to go to Africa to look after babies. It was an unusual desire and very strong. Mum home schooled me and my three siblings, and when I was about eleven my parents decided to build a little cottage out in the country. The first few years there was no power to it, so weekends in the country meant candlelight, outdoor toilets, and bread-making by hand. As a kid I didn't appreciate living off the grid, and looked forward to loading the van at the end of the weekend and going back into town, I liked the comforts. But slowly weekends turned into weeks and we stayed in the country longer. Eventually, electricity was connected and two horses were added to our lifestyle, so country life didn't seem so unappealing. I was always

Rachel Hamilton

a reserved quiet child and had a happy childhood. It wasn't until my teens I became paralyzingly insecure. At sixteen I looked twelve, at eighteen I looked fourteen and while all my peers seemed to transition into young adults overnight, I felt permanently stuck as a preteen. If the word late bloomer was created for anyone, it would have been me. I grew to hate my body and myself. My confidence was non-existent. By the time my peers were getting into relationships, I could barely even look a boy in the eyes. I felt like a freak.

I was sixteen, shy and insecure when my parents decided to move to America, so Dad could do a PhD,

It was pouring with rain on July the 10th 2007 as we boarded the first of the many flights that I would take over the next thirteen years.

"Oh, we are flying," I said excitedly to my eleven-year-old brother. The lady next to us laughed, as we were still taxing onto the runway.

Over the next eighteen months, we met many amazing people, lived in two different states, learnt about the American culture and saw the Grand Canyon, Yellow stone, Mt Rushmore and much more.

Then the crash of 2008 happened and we had to return to New Zealand. I was still shy and fearful but a spark had ignited inside me, I had fallen in love with travel.

Back in New Zealand, my insecurities began to

Courage in my Carry-On

overwhelm me, I felt lost in my silent inner battle.

Journal Entry 4th of February 2010

What's wrong with me? Why can't I be like those around me? I wish I could be anyone but me. I feel the heat of unshed tears behind my eyes, but I can't cry. I'm so sick of being invisible and unseen, it's my fault though. Please, God, I don't want to continue to isolate myself from the world. Please help me not to shut people out. I'm lost and sinking.

Deep depression set in.

Journal Entry 29th of September 2010

Life seems too much right now, I feel like I'm trapped behind a wall of fear and insecurities. As if I'm walking detached through a dream. I want to connect with people, but I can't seem too. Dear God, please change me and make me brave. I'm trying so hard to grab hold of your hand. Breathe life into me and help me see rainbow colours instead of grey. Help me to love and be loved. To be strong and see other people's pain. Teach me empathy and compassion. Change me PLEASE!!

October 2010, the year was almost over and I was finishing my Multi-Media course, I was nineteen years old but I looked fourteen, I was so fearful, it had been a stressful year filled with disappointments and I knew that something had to give, I needed to change.

Rachel Hamilton

Traveling back to NZ from USA

During my lunch break, I started typing into google, and I stumbled across a website about a ship called the Logo's Hope.

The Logos Hope is a ship that travels around the world to spread knowledge, help and hope. It does this supplying literature resources, encouraging cross-cultural understanding, training young people for more effective life and service, providing needed relief, and sharing a message of hope in God wherever there is an opportunity.

Usually, they require people to commit for two years.

Courage in my Carry-On

What caught my eye, however, was it had a three-month, short term exposure program to give a taste of life as a crew member.

Something inside me said, "Do it, take a risk, it will change everything."

So nervously I applied and a few months later on the 6th of March 2011, I arrived at the Auckland airport to catch my flight to Dubai.

I waved goodbye to my family before stepping through security, for a brief moment I paused, I was reluctant to go on, this was the door of no return.

The fear was still overwhelming as the plane took off and I would have given anything to have the plane turn back even though I knew this was something I had to do.

Fifteen hours later we touched down in Dubai, it was nothing like New Zealand; the airport was huge, with giant white marble pillars and just by walking through the airport I sensed the wealth of the United Arab Emirates. I felt intimidated by the man at customs who showed no emotion and wouldn't look me in the eyes.

The ship wasn't arriving in Dubai until the next day so I had to stay overnight in a hotel, but thankfully another New Zealander called Sarah had signed up to go on the ship, and our New Zealand contact, Dave, had connected us. We were able to get a hotel together while we waited to board the ship. Though we had only met at the airport, we soon became fast friends.

After a few hours of sleep, we ventured out for a walk. Dubai was dusty but clean. Lots of men walking around, new cars, but very few women and children.

At 3 pm we returned to the airport to join up with others about to board the Logos Hope. We had been emailed a list of people who were arriving, so we knew the names of the "Short Term team members" (or STEPPERS as we were called) and when they were arriving. Sarah and I tried to guess who they were as we waited by the arrival gate with our bags.

Then we started asking some of the jet-lagged passengers who were sitting alone, if they were joining the Logos Hope. And by this means we soon found our new team members. We got to know them a little as we waited for our ride.

I remember my first impression of the ship. It was dusk when we pulled up on the dock, as it loomed high above me, I was amazed at the huge size of it. We walked up the stairs and were thrust into life onboard a ship, with five hundred other people from all over the world.

Once our bags were put in our cabins, we were led to one of the main meeting rooms, everyone was singing and before I knew it, we were standing on the stage.

"Hey everyone, these are our new STEPPERS, guys

Courage in my Carry-On

can you introduce yourself," a man from Germany announced.

Oh boy, my comfort zone suddenly seemed VERY far away.

Remember that shy girl from New Zealand was still me, nothing miraculous happened on the plane ride to make me more outgoing.

I realised then and there I was going to have to sink or swim, figuratively I mean.

I don't remember what I said and I'm sure I stumbled and turned bright red, not my finest moment, but the start of becoming brave, nevertheless.

The next day we awoke early, ready for a busy day as the ship was to set sail for Sri Lanka. First up was orientation, learning about onboard safety and practical skills, including how to make a bed if we hit rough waters.

At 6 pm we set sail. We were told we might encounter pirates in the waters we were about to pass through, but not to tell our families at home because they would worry.

I fell asleep that night to the gentle rocking of the ship. Life had changed so much in just a few days.

The next morning a group of us rose early to see the sunrise from the top deck. Words can't describe the beauty of seeing the sun rise over nothing but water.

Days of sailing were filled with lifeboat drills, learning more about the ship-ministry and being placed in the department that we would work in six days a week until we arrived in Sri Lanka (where the ship was due to go into dry dock.)

The learning curve was steep, I was being stretched, emotionally, physically and mentally.

Journal Entry 17th of March 2011

It's tough, I want to be open with everyone here on the ship but I'm so afraid, I am thankful to be on the ship and this trip, I just want to be changed.

The Logos Hope was big. In addition to the five hundred people living on it, thousands visited at each port. There was no room for tourists aboard. Everyone had a job to do to make things run smoothly.

I was placed in the housekeeping department or "Angels" as it was called.

This meant cleaning all the public areas of the ship and doing the laundry.

It was important to keep everything extremely clean because living in such close quarters meant sickness could spread like wildfire.

Courage in my Carry-On

Sri Lanka

A few days later we arrived in Sri Lanka. I wasn't sure what to expect, I had never seen poverty before and didn't know what it would be like to be in a culture so different from mine.

The first day the ship was open to the public, I nervously went down to meet the locals on a deck set aside for it. I was still shy, but by now I was pushing myself to reach out and make connections. The Sri Lankan people are warm and friendly, and by the end of the day I felt a real connection with them, best of all they didn't seem to mind I was quieter than most. It helped that it had just been the Cricket World cup and New Zealand had played Sri Lanka and lost. So, I could always count on raising an enthusiastic banter about New Zealand's inferior cricket skills.

Rachel Hamilton

Logos Hope sailing to Sri Lanka

Courage in my Carry-On

In a corner away from the cricket fans, I noticed an old lady sitting alone. She looked so sad my heart was moved and I went to talk to her. She told me her life story and I felt privileged that she had opened up to me. Soon I met her whole family. Her daughter told me later that her mother had been very ill and she was very worried, but talking to me had helped. Me? Wow. My confidence was slowly rising.

Dry dock came. Everyone was split into groups (called challenge teams) and preparing to travel all over the country for volunteer work. For the first few weeks, I was to help out at a boys' orphanage. It had been a dream of mine for as long as I could remember to volunteer at an orphanage, so I was very excited. 3.45 am on 4th of April 2011, we caught a train. People were jammed in, hanging off the sides and stacked on the roof. We hung outside the train and felt the wind rushing past. It was an exhilarating two hours.

When we arrived at the orphanage, the boys were at school so we began clearing grass from around the yard, hot sweaty meaningful work.

The boys ranged in age from fourteen down to five years old. They knew limited English but after a game of cricket, we were able to connect.

The lush mountains surrounding the tidy buildings and

the pouring rain reminded me of home, while the staff at the home showered kindness on me.

The carer of the boys was a beautiful woman who had devoted her life to caring for the twelve boys. A kind, but firm mother figure, she was welcoming and loving to all of us volunteers as well.

I was coming out of my shell slowly but surely.

Journal Entry 9th of April 2011

We went to visit a hospital today and it had a huge effect on me. Nothing like hospitals in New Zealand. People sleeping on beds outside, dogs walking through the wards, and an undertaker next door with rows of coffins.

There is so much suffering here and yet I cannot do much about it. My head and heart are heavy.

Have you ever had your heart broken? I don't mean by a romantic relationship but by the knowledge that there are things you can't fix no matter how much you want too? I was about to have mine broken.

Caleb (not his real name) was a very cheeky sweet boy, who was always joking and trying to make us smile, he took a shine to me and wouldn't leave my side. Some of the boys still had living relatives, so the orphanage had a parent day when they would come to visit. It was exciting for the boys, but Caleb had no living relatives,

Courage in my Carry-On

so that day no one visited him.

I was sitting outside on the swing when he came to find me, he wrapped his arms around me and whispered in broken English "You be my mummy?"

My heart shattered, I was nineteen years old, in a country far away with no contact with my family. It wasn't possible, and I didn't know what to do. I pretended to not understand but instead hugged him tighter.

It was painful, I was confused, I didn't know how to process everything I was seeing, hearing, smelling and tasting.

I was also struggling with the new attention I was receiving.

Journal Entry 10th of April 2011

I feel so overwhelmed and intimidated. Back home I don't stand out, I'm quiet and I tend to blend into the background of groups, I'm not anything very special, yet here people are noticing me. I seem to stand out. People are telling me I am a hard worker, that I have good character. Yesterday someone told me everyone is talking about me and they think I fit well into the culture, they believe I should marry a Sri Lankan. Suddenly I feel under a very bright spotlight and I don't know how to handle it. I feel so vulnerable, small and insecure. Is this what being outside a comfort zone feels like? Are these the growing pains connected with inner growth and making me brave? I would give anything right now to go back to New Zealand.

I started getting headaches and wanted more than anything to go back to the ship.

Why had I come? Why had I left the comfort of home? How stupid I had been. This was just too hard. My kind teammates saw I was struggling and helped me work through some of the emotions I was feeling. Their support gave me the strength to keep reaching out to staff and children.

The rest of our days were spent with the children, clearing land and visiting hospitals and hiking up to temples, feeding monkeys and exploring more of the picture-perfect countryside.

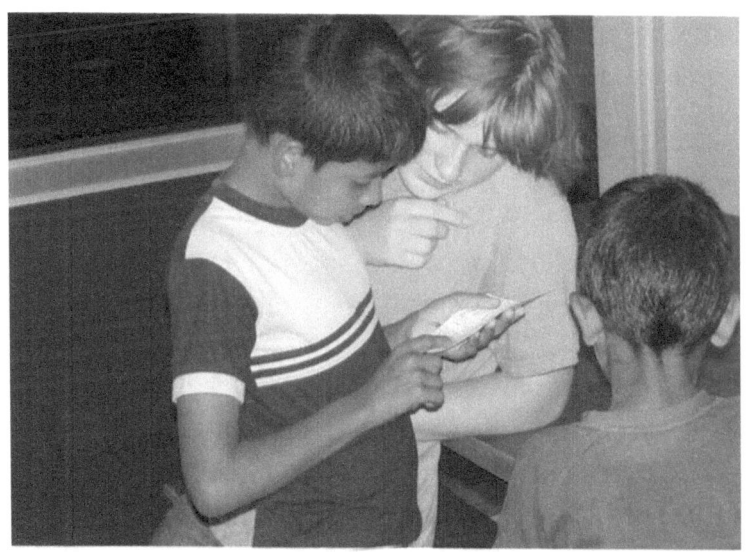

At the boys home in Sri Lanka

Courage in my Carry-On

Journal Entry 15th of April 2011

Last night we attended a funeral of the man who lived next door. He died a few days ago at the age of fifty-five. It was a stormy night, pouring with rain and pitch black as we walked to the house. We were greeted warmly by the family, as we entered the home (dimly lit by candles because the power kept going on and off.)

I found it very strange that no one was crying, even though I could tell that the family was heartbroken. We were shown into the bedroom where he lay. The lights came on for a moment, then there was a crash of thunder and the lights went out. After we had paid our respects, we were given ginger tea and biscuits. I was struck by how we were treated as honoured guests even though the family were deeply suffering. The kindness of this culture is so incredible.

The day came for us to leave; it was sad to say goodbye to the boys who we had grown to love. Even though it had only been a few weeks, it had felt like months. We arrived at the station to find our train was overbooked and there were no seats. That would have been a big problem in New Zealand, but not here. We sat on our suitcases near the open door and watched the ground pass rapidly under us the whole way back. Many people on the train came up to chat with us as not many tourists ventured into this part of the country. I didn't want to talk. So much had happened, I needed time to process it all. After the crazy train ride and an equally crazy bus ride, we arrived at the venue where we were meeting up with our shipmates, to be assigned a new Challenge Team with another group for the second part of our time on dry dock.

Standing like an Island in the middle of a sea of reuniting friends, I felt emotionally broken as flashbacks of the events, people and the cultural differences washed over me.

I had seen the realities of poverty, loss and heartbreak.

Journal Entry 19th of April 2011

This morning we left the boys home. Caleb was sad to see me go. He kept holding my hand crying and saying "you are so nice." He gave me a picture of a mother and baby and kept saying something about a mother in broken English.

It hurt my heart to leave. Now we are back at our accommodation I feel down, almost like everything is closing in on me now that all the pressure is off. Everyone else who has come back from their challenge team seems so happy and excited. Why can't I feel the same? I want to be brave.

The next day I joined my new challenge team at the

Courage in my Carry-On

train station. The group was bigger this time and our destination was nine hours away in the war-torn area of North Sri Lanka, where they were just starting to recover from the civil war.

When we arrived at the church where we were staying, I was shocked to find no beds or inside running water. There was an outdoor shower and one squat toilet for twenty people. Since we were a mixed group of male and female, we ended up developing a way of cleaning ourselves fully clothed, which caused some interesting dirt rashes. Living with twenty people, and almost no privacy had its challenges, but it was also a lot of fun.

Cleaning big wells in Sri Lanka

Rachel Hamilton

For beds, we strung two lines of mosquito netting over the hard tile floor, spread whatever blankets we had on the ground, and used our clean clothes as pillows.

Every morning we had to be up, dressed, the room tidied and the mosquito nets dismantled. All before 7 am to ensure we were out of the way of any church prayer meetings.

As there was no food provided for meals, we went out and brought food. I liked trying new foods, and I remember trying a jam called wood apple. Delicious!

The devastation of the war all around us was confronting, but like the flowers along the road, hope was blooming. I had never met such brave, kind, caring people.

Journal Entry 25th of April 2011.

You can tell this area has recently been through a war, sandbag forts scattered around the city centre. Next to the park is an army base. There are tanks and soldiers everywhere with large intimidating guns. It feels like something out of a movie.

Barbed wire is everywhere, destroyed houses, potholed roads, and spiked fences. People seem a lot more traumatised than those I stayed with during the first challenge team. Seeing all this suffering first-hand makes war no longer something I just read about. Never again will I hear of war and brush it off, because in my minds eye I will see the face of these

Courage in my Carry-On

children, who live in a hot tin shack and wear the same clothes every day, barely eating enough to survive. I'll remember the deep craters in the fields made by mines and I'll know the soldiers walking through the streets among the crumbling ruins are real. I'll think of the conversation I had with the guy who told me the war lasted thirty years and he grew up through it, as well as the woman who hasn't seen her husband for three years and isn't sure if he's dead or alive. These sights and stories are forever implanted in my memories like treasures. It's extraordinary that those who have been through pain, often have the most compassion and kindness. It touches me deeply, in a first world country we have so much, but often we complain about everything. Here they have nothing, yet they are thankful for everything.

Across the road from where we were staying was a girl's orphanage. Some of the girls on our team decided to pay a visit. I wasn't sure I wanted to go. My heart still ached for the boy's home I had left, but I decided to tag along anyway.

As we pushed the wooden gates open, beautiful girls came running towards us, that afternoon we played badminton, sang and danced with the girls and their kindness and their acceptance of total strangers left a lasting impression of how loving the Sri Lankan culture is.

Rachel Hamilton

25th of April 2011 was our first official day of work. We rose early and drove to the headquarters of the organisation we were going to help. We were assigned to work with the Alliance Development Trust.

Ariving at the Kochi docks India

The Alliance Development Trust (ADT) started its relief initiatives in the aftermath of the ethnic conflict in 1983. In 2004, when the tsunami hit Sri Lanka, ADT engaged in relief, reconstruction and development work, while helping rebuild and restore the lives of those who had lost everything to the war and tsunami.

Courage in my Carry-On

Apart from relief and development work the ADT works extensively in sustainable livelihood, education, water and sanitation (WATSAN), Sexual and Reproductive Health and Leprosy, child participation and education, disaster relief and management.

After a briefing, they took us to one of the resettlement villages which provided shelter to over three hundred people who were displaced by the war. It was a painful reminder that devastation continues long after the last shots are fired.

One of our first projects was to restore bus-stops that were dotted around the town and had fallen into disrepair. We began by clearing all the rubbish, mud and goats out of them, before scraping old posters and chipped paint off the walls. When this was done, we painted them inside and out. Once we were finished, the artists of our group painted HIV and Aids awareness slogans on them, so when people were waiting for the bus they could get more information about stopping the spread of the disease.

I enjoyed the work. It felt good to get my hands dirty and see the difference we had made. By the end of our work, there were many beautifully restored bus-stops spreading important messages. Many locals stopped by to thank us, and we fell into bed each night physically exhausted, but happy.

Some of the guys were going to clean a tube well and

they asked me to go as I had gained a reputation for being physically strong. The well (a small hole in the ground) was located inside a hospital compound. To clean it we thrust long flexible tubes deep into it and pumped high-pressure water through.

This was to flush any rubbish out. While we worked, we caught glimpses of young children in wheelchairs, which made me realise how much war can impact the lives of even the very young. Many of the patients had been paralysed by gunshot wounds. The staff were very kind and brought drinks and food to us as we worked.

The next day we climbed onto the back of a truck and headed into the country for big-well cleaning. We had been warned that around the houses and wells were active minefields, so it was extremely important to stay on the paths as many local children had died and others had lost limbs by standing on a mine. More stark realities of how recent the war was.

The big wells provided water for over two thousand families. Sadly, the water had become brown, dirty and undrinkable. The first step was to lower a pump down inside the well. It hung just above the water. While the well was being drained, we jumped ten or fifteen feet down into the water, grabbed hold of ropes and scraped the sides of the well clean with coconut skins. Once the well was empty, we dug the mud off the bottom and loaded it into buckets that were pulled to the top. We

Courage in my Carry-On

got out a similar way by walking up the smooth sides clinging to long ropes. It was not for the faint hearted and it was best not to look down. I felt empowered as I used my upper body strength to climb out. My adventurous spirit was emerging.

The sun was scorching and we had water, so what better way to cool off than with a water fight. I found myself relaxing, adapting and opening up more to those in my team and the Sri Lankan's.

After a long fun day, we headed back to the church, stopping at a lake for a swim. It had been a successful, worthwhile day. Two thousand families now had clean drinking water.

The local Sri Lankan's we worked alongside were the kindest people you could ever meet. They have given their whole lives to help those affected by war. Many got up at 5 o'clock every morning to hand out food so children wouldn't go hungry. Many faced terrible pain but had risen and become amazing men and woman of God.

Days spent cleaning wells, bus-stops and painting schools made the weeks fly by. Our time was drawing to a close.

On our last night, we were picked up and taken to a secret location. We did not know where we were going. When we arrived, we found ourselves honoured guests at an army base, where we were welcomed by the top commander. As we sat around eating cake and sipping sweet tea, he thanked us for everything we had done, and presented us with a small trophy with our names on it and the nationalities we represented. I'll never forget the moment he asked:

"Where is the New Zealander?"

Everyone pointed to me. I felt self-conscious but honoured that I had been singled out. For the next hour, we sang a few songs with the army and then made our way back to the church to pack, for we were returning to the ship the next day.

The pastor's wife got up early the next morning to make us sweet tea before we left. As we hugged our new friends, we were sad to say goodbye, but also excited to catch up with our other shipmates back at the dock. The thought of a REAL shower after using an outside bucket for two weeks, kept us going during our nine-hour journey back. We joked about the first two things that we were going to do once we got back on the ship; have a shower and lie on a REAL bed.

Arriving back inside the ship after five weeks was like coming home. There was much hugging and laughing as we reunited with friends. We all had fascinating stories to exchange.

Settling back into the routine of housekeeping on the

Courage in my Carry-On

ship was difficult and I struggled with the mundaneness of it. The last five weeks had been an adventure, and each day held something new. Once again, I was struggling to work through everything emotionally. I worked from 6 am-3:30 pm five days a week but I felt I was no longer making a difference.

The ship was to sail to India as soon as we arrived back, but a few more things needed to be done, so we spent two more weeks in Sri Lanka. It was nice to have the chance to explore Colombo a bit more, as it's a major city, unlike the small towns and villages we had explored during the last five weeks.

I had grown to love the culture and the kindness of the Sri Lankan people

Working every day with people from all over the world expanded my world view and taught me a lot about different cultures, while the two Challenge Teams expanded my friends. I was still one of the quietest on the ship, but I was learning to interact more. It was nice waking up every morning and chatting with like-minded people over breakfast, lunch, and dinner.

I decided to ask if I could work in the engine for a couple of shifts as I wanted a taste of working in the heart of the ship. To my delight, they said yes, and I was given overalls to wear. It was hot, loud and draining work. I crawled around on my hands and knees as I cleaned oil off the floor. It was a hard slog, but I loved doing something else that I might never have the chance to do again.

New Zealand flag

May 23, 2011. At 9:40 pm we set sail for India. I stood on the upper deck watching the port that had been our home for nine weeks, get smaller and smaller. I had come to make a difference in the lives of the people of

Courage in my Carry-On

Sri Lanka, but they were the ones who made a difference in me. Their gentle simple kind way of living taught me so much. Through them, I saw the true power of prayer, real servant hood, and the value of practising gratitude in all situations. I was slowly learning to love and accept myself as I realised that differences are OK.

Rachel Hamilton

India

Due to the ship being in Dry dock longer than expected, I wasn't going to have much time in India before I flew home. India was on my list of places to visit and I feel so blessed I got to see it. I had grown close to some of the Indian volunteers on the ship and I felt their excitement almost as my own, as the Kochi docks came into view.

India was a shock to all the senses, the bright colours, smells, sounds, and taste were overpowering. The culture was similar to Sri Lanka with a few small differences; like more English was spoken in India, and the colours were extremely vibrant.

The ship opened to the public, and soon long lines of people were patiently waiting to board the ship. I went down to connect with locals and out of nowhere a large group of wide-eyed children crowded around me.

Courage in my Carry-On

"Sing, dance and talk some more," they shouted, giggling.

I felt like a celebrity and enjoyed making them laugh and smile.

One girl stood out. Sarah was a sweet fourteen-year-old. She came and sat next to me in a quiet moment, and opened up about her dream of one day travelling aboard the ship. Just before she left, she begged me to never forget her, and to this day I often think of her and pray that her dreams will come true.

My last day arrived. It was very emotional to say goodbye to everyone, as the time onboard the Logos Hope had been life-changing. I had learnt so much about the outside world, who I was, and what I was capable of doing. It was the beginning of the change I had desperately begged God for.

Rachel Hamilton

Home from Sea

Returning home from the ship was surreal, I had changed, but everything at home felt the same. I was so worried that I would go back to the old me.

Although my mentors on the ship had explained re-entry was going to be hard, I did not expect it to be as frustrating as it was. I was angry at my culture and how selfish and entitled everyone seemed to be.

I was still quiet but not so insecure as I had been, and I was keen to travel again.

One day I got the news a close friend of mine had taken her own life. We were both a few months off our 21st birthdays.

It shook me deeply I felt myself retreating right back into the fearful girl I used to be.

Courage in my Carry-On

Guilt held me in a vice grip. If only I had reached out and asked the right questions. If I wasn't so quiet, maybe she would have opened up to me and still be alive.

I felt it was my fault and I hated myself for it. Eventually, the grip of guilt eased but it took a long time.

To this day my friend is never far from my thoughts, she has forever changed the way I see the world and I aim to always be kind, because I never truly know what battles those around me are silently fighting. It's heartbreaking to know my friend was hurting so much suicide seemed the only relief.

Dearest reader if you are struggling, know that you are so very important, and this pain is temporary. Life will get better, I promise.

Please, please, remember suicide is never the answer.

Rachel Hamilton

Nightmare

Three months went by, I got a job as a live-in Nanny for a family that lived three hours away from my hometown. I was excited. I loved children and was pleased for the opportunity to gain some independence. As an added bonus, there was free accommodation, which would enable me to save money. I packed my suitcases with toys and presents for the kids and set off for a week's training.

Right from the beginning there were signs something was wrong with this family. The first spot of trouble was when the woman refused to pick me up from the hotel at the end of my induction with the organisation that was overseeing us Nanny's. I was in a strange city and it was not an unreasonable request, as she did not live miles and miles away, yet she insisted I find way to her house by bus. And when I got lost and called for

Courage in my Carry-On

directions, she screamed abuse over the phone at me.

How naïve I was.

Finally, she calmed down enough to arrange a meeting place. Holding tightly to my two suitcases I nervously walked along the road. Once I got there and settled in, things went from bad to worse, it was the longest six weeks of my life. The verbal and emotional abuse I suffered still gives me nightmares. Day after day she worked me to the bone, paying me for twenty hours but working me at least sixty plus hours.

She screamed at me when I didn't do the washing but when I put a load on without being asked, she accused me of using all their resources up. She told me that I must always have the house spotless even though she had multiple young children.

One day when I couldn't handle the stress, I drove home for my weekend off, leaving a note saying I had gone. When I returned on Sunday, the punishments began. Shouting, cold looks, not speaking to me, and explaining in detail the abusive things she felt like doing to people who did things she didn't like. The days dragged on endlessly as if time stood still. I woke in terror each day, afraid of the violent mood swings. She was pleasant one moment and abusive the next.

One day my caseworker came for a meeting to check how I was performing. I sat in silence as my employer told lie after lie, tearing me down in the hopes of getting something for nothing.

"Rachel never does any work," she lied, "I'm paying her too much and I'm going to cut her pay down."

I could see the caseworker was on her side because the Nanny organization made money by placing me in a home.

I held back tears as the truth sank in; no one was going to stick up for me and I couldn't stand up for myself. After the tirade was over, my caseworker took me into the other room.

"You must apologise and work harder," she said. Then she left.

It was like being in an exploitive cult. After I apologised, I sat alone in my room, tears streaming down my cheeks. I had never felt so trapped and hopeless in my life. I felt there was no way I could leave, as the mind control was so strong, it had placed chains in my head.

One night they had a drunken party. My room was in the basement, off the room where all the men were drinking and smoking. I stayed upstairs afraid to go down as they were very drunk, and I did not feel safe. Despite this, I was told I had to go down to my bedroom, even though my room had no lock on the door. I knew I was very vulnerable, so as the party went on, I prayed that God would keep me safe and protect me from anyone

Courage in my Carry-On

coming into my room, which he did.

Weeks passed, during which time, my parents became concerned for my wellbeing and tried to persuade me to leave. But the level of emotional abuse I was experiencing, made me terrified of what could happen if I tried to leave.

Finally, my parents convinced me to go home with them. But even at home the torment in my mind continued, fear shot through me every time the phone rang, I became sick with the stress and the doctor wrote me a medical certificate stating I was unfit to go back.

I will never be able to thank my parents enough for getting me out of there. I still struggle today with the side effects of the emotional damage inflicted by that woman.

Because of her, I have anxiety in many workplace situations. I fear making mistakes and being shouted at. I struggle to have healthy workplace relationships or drop my emotional guard. It's not all bad, however, through it I have been given the gift of empathy and compassion.

Once I had recovered from my nannying job enough to venture out of my comfort zone again, an opportunity came up in Australia to do a short course through Flight centre. This is it I thought! A perfect way to travel and still make money. I decided to become a travel agent.

Rachel Hamilton

Sickness

On the morning I set off for Australia, I sat in the airport waiting for the boarding call for my flight. At last it came. I rubbed my lower back as I stood in line with my passport ready, my joints had been aching for days but I didn't take much notice.

"Stop complaining body," I muttered to myself, "don't interfere with my adventure."

After I arrived, I stayed with a friend of the family and started the course early the next morning, catching the bus at 7 am into downtown Sydney. The next two weeks were quite stressful, I didn't know why, but I found it hard to focus on the training and the four hour a day commute was a killer. My feet were so painful I took the maximum dosage of Panadol and Ibuprofen that it was safe to take, but it didn't make a difference. Then my feet started swelling and sleep became impossible.

Courage in my Carry-On

Somehow, I managed to pass the course and I was back at the airport again, grateful to be going home. My back and shoulders throbbed as I clicked my seat belt on and settled back for the three-hour plane trip to New Zealand.

Feeding monkeys in Sri Lanka

Things got worse once I got home. Every day the pain grew more unbearable until I was hardly able to move. Even the smallest movement shot sharp pains into my joints, it felt like tiny shards of glass cutting into my bones, while a deep unrelenting ache settled all over my body. I lay in bed at night with tears, slipping down my face as I tried not to scream in agony. The pain was the

Rachel Hamilton

worst I had ever felt in my life.

Thousands of thoughts ran through my head. Why was I in so much pain? Did I have cancer? I withdrew from everyone and everything. No matter what I took, relief was always out of reach.

My worried Mum took me to see doctors time and time again, but they had no idea what was wrong with me. I felt so out of it, all I wanted was to be pain-free. Then the long road of tests began, each one coming back negative. Still no one knew what I was suffering from. Eventually, after many weeks I was called back into the doctors.

"We have found something in your blood tests that is worrying." the kind doctor said, "your inflammation marker is high."

After more tests I received the official diagnosis; Rheumatoid Arthritis. An autoimmune disease. Symptoms include fatigue, pain and swelling in the joints. It is a long-term chronic pain condition that has no cure but with the right medication can be controlled.

Chronic pain is a phrase I never expected to understand intimately. It is a word that holds many burdens. Chronic pain sufferers the world over, are united by an unwanted companion who never leaves our side, and life is never the same again. The ship made me push my limitations, now my illness taught me how to live within them. Though I didn't understand it at the time, I now see this was another step in my journey towards becoming brave, not fun like an overseas trip, but just as important.

Oh, how deeply frustrating that year was. I had to come to grips with my new 'normal,' of doctor's appointments, and daily medications. I felt so alone, my parents (understandably) didn't want me to have a future of pain, so, they hoped it was all in my head.

They tried to get me to stop focusing on it. I hated myself and my body that had turned against me. Suddenly my hopes and dreams were crashing down. I was twenty-one years old and now travel seemed an unreachable dream.

I also felt ashamed because arthritis seemed an old person's disease. Moreover, I had seen the photos of disfigured hands and feet. So, although I struggled with daily pain and the side effects of the medications, I told very few people outside my family. At long last, after months of tests, painful treatments, and hospital waiting rooms, I was on the right medication. My life has become manageable again. Sure, pain is still there, but I am able to function and have most of my movement back.

In 2014 Dad got a job in Australia, and the company was willing to pay for the whole family to relocate. Even though it wasn't solo and I was twenty-two, it was still travel and a chance to live in another culture. We packed the contents of our house into a container and flew to Sydney to start a new life.

I like to think of New Zealand and Australia as cousins, in Australia I have all the comforts of home with the added excitement of being a "foreigner," or the one with the "thick accent." I love how weird birds laugh at me, and am thrilled to see Kangaroo meat alongside Marmite and Vegemite in the supermarkets. Even the flag flying in the wind looks almost like the New Zealand flag.

I feel privileged that I can work in Australia without the worry of a visa because of our two countries' special agreement.

But the flip side is, I had forgotten how much upheaval is involved with moving countries. Even the little things you take for granted like a library card, bank account, driver's licence, mobile phone, and doctor, all have to be replaced.

And even though the two cultures are similar, it's still possible to experience culture shock. The money and social cues are different. In New Zealand, it's very common to pop round to someone's house to say hi, but in Australia, we found it was socially correct to make an appointment first.

Now that my daily pain was manageable, and I was

Courage in my Carry-On

monitored by a local rheumatologist. I set about finding a job, and got one as a housekeeper in a luxury resort ten minutes from home. The money was great and I grew to love the tight-knit team. Slowly my love for travel and pushing myself outside my comfort zones started to fade.

I was known and liked by everyone at work, (a strange feeling for me who so often merged into the background.) Each day I felt excited to go to work. I was comfortable, secure, liked, and valued. I was given more responsibility than older co-workers. My plans for earning good money and saving for a house were becoming a reality.

There was only one problem, there was no growth, I was slowly getting stuck in a rut. Don't get me wrong, I think it's great to love your job and make good money, but for my personal growth, I was at a stalemate. So, I pushed my deep desire of new cultures and adventures away and settled into an unhealthy place of working twelve-hour days, sometimes sixteen days in a row. I was burning out and I didn't even know it.

Then the workplace bullying started. I was fragile from what had happened in New Zealand, so I took it personally. I was very stressed, but for months I clung to my job until one day I returned home from work and couldn't stop shaking. Because of my health condition, I knew I had to quit before I did more damage to my body. So, I went back an hour later and quit. At the time it was devastating.

In a single moment, my world crashed. I sat in the car and cried uncontrollably, I couldn't believe I had let someone bully me again, though I didn't realise it at the time something deep down inside me changed. I had actively taken back control of my life and never again would I lie down and let myself be a victim. I lost my job but won a massive inner battle.

Courage in my Carry-On

Cambodia

Months passed, I didn't get another job, but I reconnected with my love of travel. I decided to go overseas again. As usual, I spurned the typical tourist destination. This time I booked a flight to Thailand and Cambodia. I was to travel with an organisation that rescues children who are being sexually trafficked or at risk for it.

Why did I choose to go with an organisation that deals with human trafficking?

Because I had to know how pain, courage, and hope are intertwined.

I wrote this on my blog weeks before I flew out.

Just over a week until I go on another solo trip, I'm terrified. More afraid than when I was nineteen and I left for three months, travelling to three different countries while living on a ship.

I'm only going for two weeks and yet this is one of the scariest things I have ever done.

Why, because I'm going to see things I don't want to see, things that I want to pretend don't happen.

See lives I cannot reach, hearts I cannot heal, evils I cannot defeat.

I like my comfort zone, the big safe walls of apathy. A safe, clean place where slavery is something I just read about.

I don't want to see the broken abused and crushed. The faces of children who have been touched by more evil than I could even begin to imagine.

But I have to go, I have to know.

It was hot and humid when I stepped into the dusty streets of Cambodia a week later. Because I had been on the Logos Hope, I was no stranger to poverty, humidity and dust, but I sensed something in this beautiful country; deep and raw suffering. Pain that time had not yet healed.

Cambodia has a dark, brutal past. Two million people died under Pol Pots hand. Under his rule Cambodia lost it's highly educated people and its educational system.

It was hard to comprehend that the majority of the

Courage in my Carry-On

brothel customers were not overseas tourists but local men, a painful self-destructive way of life.

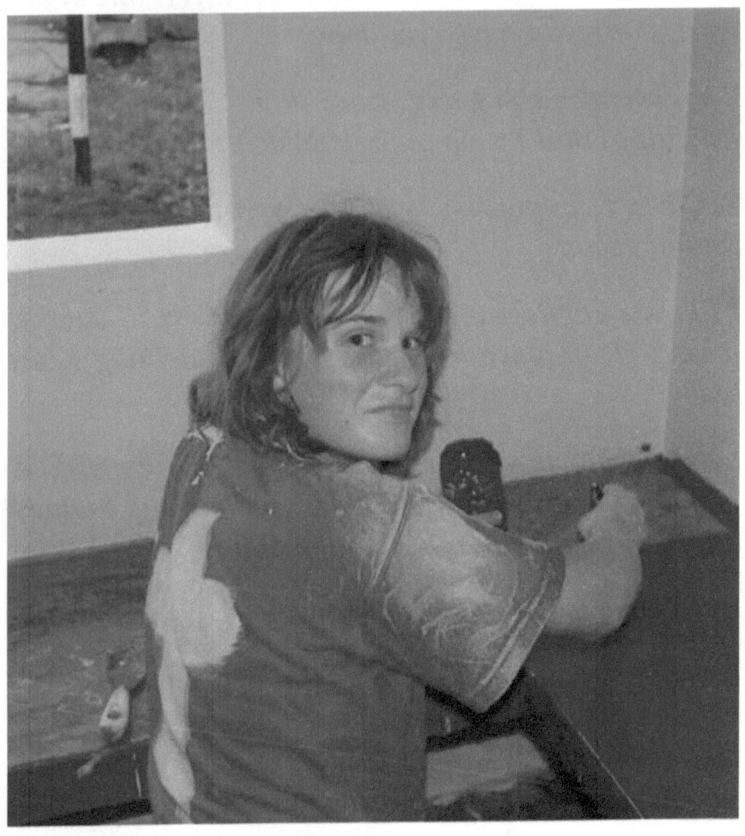

Cleaning bus stops Sri Lanka

Written into the beliefs of the culture is the attitude that children exist for their parent's benefit and women exist for men's pleasure and benefit.

Rachel Hamilton

Cambodian daughters are considered property. They are there to provide income for the family.

A well-known saying is that men are like gold and women are like cloth. Drop gold in the dirt, you can wash it clean, but if you drop cloth, the stain never comes out.

From this comes the deep shame and social disgrace of the women who have been forced into sex work.

Messed up family trees with decades of abuse have distorted the country's view.

Because child trafficking has become less obvious in the last few years, valid statistics are harder to come by, but the under-ground business is thriving.

Criminals are able to continue because they adapt with the law changes and times. Girls are taken to the doctors to get a certificate of virginity and then taken by their mothers to hotels and brothels.

Heavy stuff, right?

Fortunately, I had a wonderful group of people to share this journey with.

Though none of us had met before arriving in Cambodia we soon became a close team, forging lasting friendships.

The group leader was called Lynda and from the moment I saw her I knew she was going to change my life in some

Courage in my Carry-On

way. Her energy, compassion and love were catchy. Although she probably will never know it, she made an impact on everyone in our team. Her greatest desire was to spread the word about child sexual exploitation, and show us the hope and healing the rescued girls had found through the power of God's love.

Her eyes swam with tears when she talked of the moment her eyes were opened to the heartbreaking realities of child slavery. Her concern was so great, she and her family left behind their comforts and learnt how to adapt to a new culture.

After settling in, one of the first places we visited was the Tuol Sleng Genocide Museum and the Killing fields. Of all the things I have seen in my travels, this was the most confronting.

The Tuol Sleng Genocide Museum located in the middle of Phnom Penh was the interrogation and detention centre during the Khmer Rouge regime. Its innocent beginnings as a high school, turned deadly in 1975 when the buildings became the hub for the prison system throughout the country. It was used for the detention, interrogation, torture and extermination of those deemed intellectual, due to Pol Pot's attempts to create a Cambodian "master race" through social engineering.

Merely wearing glasses or the ability to speak a foreign language could have you executed. Because of the policy of guilt-by-association, whole families of 'political enemies' were detained at the centre. Only twelve former inmates survived out of over twenty thousand prisoners. Four of them were children. Most of the inmates were photographed and their interrogations recorded.

We were all silent as we walked through the eerie rooms of the museum. Knowing we were standing where unspeakable suffering had taken place shook us all. Photographs of the horrors, including bodies chained to bed frames with pools of wet blood underneath, were hung on the walls, along with heartbreaking photos of thousands of prisoners.

As humans, we often try to distance ourselves from suffering. We search for differences between ourselves and victims of horrors so we can cling to the belief that it couldn't happen to us. As I walked through the rooms, I saw the faces of those who died, but only when I stumbled across Kerry Hamill's photo, did the reality hit home.

Kerry Hamill was a twenty-six-year-old New Zealander who was innocently sailing around the world when his yacht was blown off course in a storm. He was captured and sent to Tuol Sleng. Westerners were singled out and tortured until they admitted to being CIA spies. He was just one year older than me, and guilty of nothing more than being in the wrong place at the wrong time, yet he died.

We continued the painful journey to the killing fields at Cheoeung Ek. This was where many of the prisoners were taken. When we got there, we were given an audio device to wear. Most of the time when you go to a tourist destination, people are talking, but here everyone was quiet, small groups of people walked together, some were crying. The air was thick with sorrow and there were no smiles. The voice of the audio spoke in my ear as I walked past markers that showed mass graves. One sobering sign said:

MASS GRAVE OF MORE THAN 100 VICTIMS, CHILDREN AND WOMEN WHO MAJORITY WERE NAKED.

Another sign said:

MASS GRAVE OF 166 VICTIMS WITHOUT HEADS.

I felt guilty for my lack of suffering when I read those words. These people had been robbed of dignity, even in death.

Not far away I saw a tree glittering in the sun, when I walked up to it, I saw it was covered in brightly coloured bracelets. The sign beside it read:

KILLING TREE AGAINST WHICH EXECUTIONERS BEAT CHILDREN.

Rachel Hamilton

I felt the breath leave my body in a gasp as the audio told of the children and infants who were smashed to death against the tree. The soldiers who did these atrocious things, laughed as they killed the children in front of their mothers. They laughed to prove they were tough for they feared becoming targets themselves.

I stood and stared at the sign, aware that metres away from me, tiny babies were murdered.

My tears fell as I walked to the building in the middle of the field and looked at thousands of skulls stacked on top of each other. Men, women, children, each with their own story, their hopes and dreams destroyed, their dignity stolen.

We were all subdued that night when we returned to the hotel; I had had my heartbroken for the second time, my eyes opened wide to the suffering of this world. As we struggled to come to grips with the horror we had seen, Lynda explained to us, it was important to visit these places to give us an understanding of the history and brokenness of Cambodia.

The next day we went to meet some young girls who had been rescued from sex trafficking. I was nervous, but to my surprise we were met by the most beautiful girls, by looking at them you would never have guessed the pain they had suffered. We spent the morning painting nails, dancing and laughing. While I sat quietly (letting the more outgoing in our group talk) a young girl came

Courage in my Carry-On

and sat next to me, she had beautiful long dark hair and the most radiant smile, her courage and dignity after everything she had been through, shone brightly.

That afternoon we were taken to visit a village out in the country, where the houses were built high off the ground to protect them from flooding. Though we had been told to only drink bottled water, we were offered flavoured shaved ice and for a moment I forgot and took a bite.

By dinner time I felt strangely unsettled in the stomach. So, while the rest of the group chatted, I excused myself and went to bed, for we had to wake early the next morning as we were travelling to Siam Reap, eight hours away. I hoped I could sleep off whatever it was that was troubling my stomach. But no sooner did I lay down than I was up and vomiting.

Danielle my roommate arrived back.

"I hope you feel better soon," she said looking concerned.

"Thanks," I groaned.

I vomited on and off until I drifted into a restless sleep. I was awakened by the sound of more vomiting. But this time it was Danielle not me.

Oh dear, we struggled through that night. Lynda came to check on us, and once again her golden heart and genuine care shone through her selfless offer as she said:

"You can wake me at any time of the night if you get worse."

By the time morning arrived, I had not vomited for a few hours but I was too afraid to eat anything. Danielle and I climbed onto the bus feeling weak. "Don't throw up," I said to myself over and over.

I didn't, but the bumpy long trip was agony to my already rolling stomach. Although beautiful scenery flew past, I was too preoccupied to notice.

Halfway we stopped by the side of the road to try Kralanh (sticky rice cooked in coconut milk and black-eyed peas stuffed in bamboo.) My stomach still didn't feel good, but I ate a small amount.

At last, we arrived at our new hotel, I was happy to get into bed, and I fell asleep soon after. Thankfully I woke up the next day feeling heaps better.

In Siem Reap, we visited more rescue homes and met more courageous girls. One of the seven wonders of the world, Angkor Wat, is located in this area. Angkor Wat is an ancient temple built between 1113 and 1150 A.D, and not to be missed. Of course, we were all excited to see it. Early in the morning we climbed into Tuktuks and made our way.

It was sunrise when we arrived, and to say it was

Courage in my Carry-On

beautiful is an understatement. All the heaviness I had felt in the last few days washed away with one look at the sun rising over the magnificent and ancient temples.

It was one of those moments you pinch yourself and think, am I really here?

We spent the wandering through the gigantic ruins and it was an incredible experience.

All too soon our time in Cambodia ended and it was time to head to Thailand. We hugged Lynda and waved goodbye.

Once more a culture had shaken, moulded and stretched me.

Rachel Hamilton

Thailand

Thailand in many ways was similar to Cambodia; both have a lot of history, both are humid, and the languages sound similar.

Our guides took us to the red-light district in Bangkok. Why you may ask? Because while trafficking in Cambodia is more hidden and the demand is more from locals, sex tourism is what fuels most of the demand in Thailand. The organisation wanted us to see the realities of it.

It was late at night and as we drove to the district, I became more nervous.

We got out of the cars and walked into the outdoor area that was lined with brothels. That's when I saw HER and we made eye contact. I was surrounded by hundreds of people, but all I saw was IIER. She was dressed in a

Courage in my Carry-On

skimpy suggestive outfit, yet when she spoke, I could see she was a girl just like me. A girl who most likely grew up dreaming of prince charming, a man that would hold her and love her, respect, protect, and marry her. Maybe she was a little girl who just wanted to be a wife and mum when she grew up.

Those years of innocence were long gone. Night after night as she sold herself to men who abused her and misused her, she was forced to give away something that should only be given to a loving husband. She said hello and asked me how I was, a plastic smile plastered to her face, pain flicking in her eyes. I could sense the loneliness and betrayal behind the bright blue mascara.

I managed to smile and say hello, but it was with difficulty, because that was the moment sex trafficking became a reality to me. This girl's life could have been my destiny if I had been born into different circumstances. Although we talked as two normal young women, I was free but she was not. It was wrong, we both should have been free.

As we moved down the street, invisible chains of bondage were everywhere. They coiled around the beautiful girls trapped in slavery by the needs of their family, subject through powerlessness, to the threats and abuse of their pimps and brothel owners. As I walked up a set of stairs, I passed an older man in his fifties standing next to a petite girl barely out of her teens, as he bent to kiss her, I heard him whisper the words:

"How much?"

She lifted two trembling fingers.

"2000 Bart."

Red hot anger burnt through me. I wanted to punch him hard, grab the girl and run far from this terrible place of cruelty and hopelessness. This was pure evil and I could do nothing to stop it.

White Temple Thailand

I spotted another man. He was around my age and in another time and place, I would have said he was good looking. Maybe he was from Europe, Australia or even

Courage in my Carry-On

New Zealand, who knows. Why had he come? Did his twisted need of fulfilment bring him here? What pushed him to sink this low, to force a girl to sell her most treasured gift and dignity for nothing in return, no commitment, no wedding ring. I felt hatred, but also gut-wrenching pity. Maybe his father was never around. Deep down did he feel worthless, so he continued to hunt for a place of belonging? Did he know that this quest for pleasure came at the expense of someone's freedom?

At that moment I was hit with the realisation that sex trafficking is a tragedy for the women trapped in it, but the men that create the demand lose something too. These men are caught in a web of self-destruction; the slippery slope of dehumanisation. Which distorts the image of real intimacy and love. This wasn't love or intimacy, but short-term fulfilment of a lustful desire, with the price tag of years of soul-crushing torment for the victims. Something had to be done.

That night it took a long time to fall asleep.

A few days later we went to visit one of the Prevention Homes, places where children are placed if they are at risk of being forced into slavery and sexual exploitation.

We played soccer and walked around the beautiful gardens. Out of one of the bedrooms bounded the cutest little girl I had ever seen. Her face was bright with innocence, as she pulled at my hand and begged to show me something special. We did not speak the same language, but we shared an understanding.

In her short brown hair, her cheeky grin, again I saw myself, the little girl with boundless energy.

This beautiful angel was protected from the evils I had seen. Thank God for that. Her eyes were so alive, and her heart undamaged.

We sat on a blanket in the sun and she began creating me a feast of plastic food.

My heart rejoiced as I covered my pretend pizza in imaginary tomato sauce.

This was so pure and right, a child, free to be a child.

This beautiful girl has become my motivation, my inspiration.

I will always try to do my part to protect and nurture innocence.

After our visit we visited another home. This home was for girls who had been rescued and were pregnant or had a baby.

Rebekah (not her real name) spoke in a trembling voice of the hope she had found in Jesus Christ. Through the courageous men who rescued her from the brothel, she saw God's hands and feet. Before she was rescued her life had been nothing but pain but as she learnt about

Courage in my Carry-On

God's love, her eyes danced with newfound hope, she had found the strength to rise above her past.

Rebekah came to talk to me. As she spoke, her arm stroked my shoulder and love bubbled out of her. Before my eyes, she blossomed in the warmth of my kindness, as she embraced and accepted my love. It convicted me that this girl had been through so much abuse and yet was so open to accepting love and prepared to share her true self (insecurities and all) while I, who had experienced nothing like her pain, was so bound up, terrified to show even the smallest part of my heart.

I had built my identity on being strong, responsible, and tough, to the point I was drowning in the shallow waters of my loneliness. I wanted to be the one to listen and be there for those around me, but I didn't want to let anyone into my life. I was learning about myself through these beautiful, brave girls.

The last few days were filled with touristy things. I sailed on boats, rode elephants, and held a big snake. Then before I knew it, it was time to head to the airport.

Goodbyes never get easier no matter how many times you do them. As I hugged all my new friend's goodbye, I was happy that they were all from Australia so there was a chance we would see each other again.

I wrote on my blog when I arrived home.

Rachel Hamilton

26th of January 2016.

The night after I arrived home from Thailand, 12 am and the tears are flowing.

I am so broken from the things I have seen, looking into the face of the beautiful young girl who has seen more evil in her childhood than most people see in their whole lifetime.

I can't imagine the rejection and betrayal she must have felt to be sold to a brothel by her parents.

How could I comprehend that the very same hotel we stayed in, had private rooms where such evil could be done to an underage girl in secret?

I have walked through a red-light district trying not to cry as I hurried past hundreds of women trapped in unspeakable pain, helpless to do anything to set them free.

Evil was thick in the air and the chains of despair could almost be seen.

How painful it is to have your eyes open to the darkest of evil.

I can't go back to who I was before, not after these sights.

But more than that, I have seen the joy, hope, light and restoration in the eyes of the girls who have been

Courage in my Carry-On

rescued from hopelessness.

I have seen the power of God who breaks every chain of shame and guilt and brings these brave girls into a place of true freedom.

I felt passionate about everything I had seen in Thailand and Cambodia. I wanted to do my part to make a difference and create change. I decided I wanted to pack up and move to Thailand. So, I found a job at a local hotel and started to save money.

While I worked, I contacted a few organisations, and for a time everything seemed to be falling into place. But remember how from a young age I wanted to go to Africa and look after babies? The pull to Africa that bubbled underground during my childhood, rose to the surface again as my plans for volunteering in Thailand fell through. I started googling missions and found an organisation that looks after orphans and widows in Uganda. Best of all, they also had a Babies Home where they accepted international volunteers without any special qualifications. I applied and they accepted me. At last, I was going to Africa for three months to help look after babies. My childhood dream was about to come true.

Rachel Hamilton

Uganda

Once again, I was alone in a foreign airport. It was hot and sticky on the 13th of December 2016 when I stood at Customs in the Entebbe airport; the man stamped my passport and now I was officially in Uganda.

When the doors opened to the outside world, bright sunlight hit my eyes, I felt dazed but excited.

That's when I first met Freddo. From the moment I met him, I instantly felt like I had gained the older brother I always wanted. I was jet-lagged, probably looked and smelt awful. Yet he welcomed me warmly.

The drive to the hotel where I was staying was about an hour away but due to the heavy traffic it took longer. That was OK, though because Freddo went out of his

Courage in my Carry-On

way to put me at ease. Working with the organisation for over ten years, he was no stranger to internationals who arrive along with their unique qualities and challenges. He had a special gift for making many people feel supported and appreciated.

As we moved along the crowded roads, my eyes took in the beautiful view that is typical of Uganda; the bright red dirt, the colourful roadside markets.

After dropping me at the hotel and making sure I was comfortable and safe, Freddo left.

The hotel was located in the middle of Kampala, where the majority of the international volunteers lived.

I got to know the other volunteers as I settled in. It felt like I was living in a mini United Nations, as we were from all over the world. New Zealand, USA, Canada, Japan, Hong Kong and more. I was thrilled to meet Melody who I had randomly connected with through Instagram before arriving.

As with every other country I have visited, I was excited to see the strange-looking money. In Uganda the currency is shillings and four hundred dollars is about one million shillings. I thought it was so cool being able to say I was a millionaire when I withdrew money from the ATM.

Rachel Hamilton

At the Equator in Uganda

Courage in my Carry-On

Uganda has been through difficult times and you can see the aftermath of that pain and struggle, but oh what beauty has been born from the ashes.

You will never meet more kind, beautiful, lovely people.

There is a joy, sweetness and compassion in this country that is so inspiring.

Life was wonderful, daily I enjoyed rich hospitality, wonderful food and loving community.

After Cambodia and Thailand, Uganda was a lot easier for me to adjust to because English is one of the main languages.

The hotel we lived at was not far from downtown Kampala, we lived in a special wing created specifically for volunteers, complete with a self-contained kitchen and private living room.

The first week flew by in a jet-lagged haze. The days started with catching a bus for a one-hour journey to the Babies Home in the country.

The manager of the Babies Home was a woman called Vicky, and strangely I first met her not at the Babies Home but when I sat waiting for the bus. She is a beautiful woman who you could only describe as a lady by the way she walks, talks, and interacts with those around her. She is everything I hope to be. She is kind, strong, capable and wise.

Rachel Hamilton

I was instantly struck by the way she made the volunteers feel loved, accepted and supported. We soon became fast friends and even though she juggled so much responsibility, she always made time to chat with me. She taught me what true leadership is.

I wrote on my blog:

I have only been in Uganda just over a week and I am struggling to put into words how deeply this place has impacted me.

How do I describe how wonderful it is to have a life-long dream come true?

For as long as I can remember I have dreamed of working with children in Africa.

For a week it has been my reality.

Yet I feel so unworthy, why was I chosen to hold, love, and help care for these priceless children.

I honestly don't know.

But when I hold these beautiful babies, look deep into their eyes and see hope rise from pain. I cry. Tears of hope. I see a God who rescues, redeems and lifts the forgotten to a mountain top.

My days aren't all hugs and kisses. They are filled with dirty diapers, babies who don't want to eat, tears, cleaning, and my arms ache from rocking tired

Courage in my Carry-On

babies, who don't want to sleep. But right now, there is nothing more fulfilling or wonderful.

This time instead of being broken, my heart was slowly being healed.

How do I put into words how truly grateful I am for the time I am spending in Africa?

I can't.

A magical place where little lives are formed.

Each morning when I arrive at work, I am greeted by smiles, hugs and little voices shouting, "Mamma"

I start by making the beds and helping dress them.

Then they have family time and playtime.

When the babies arrive here, they are placed into families with a nanny and five other babies. The nanny is the mother figure who for the first two years of their life raises them as her own. When they turn two, they are adopted into the village.

I am so inspired by the nannies for the way they care and love the babies.

We often sit outside in the sun.

Then it's lunchtime, feeding twenty-plus babies per room is a mission, but somehow it works out.

Rachel Hamilton

The toddlers so cute when they close their eyes and put their hands together for the prayer.

There are five different rooms, currently, I am in the small toddler's room.

I have been with the babies who are six to ten months old and the older babies who are ten to eighteen months.

International volunteers change rooms every two weeks.

After lunch, we get a two-hour break because the babies are having an afternoon nap.

During this time, I often walk down to the nearby village and talk to the children or join the babies in sleep.

When we come back from the break, it's time for a snack and bible time.

Then it's playtime again.

You will never find more loving little people than these babies.

Each day I am overwhelmed by the love they shower on me.

Tight hugs, kisses, little arms wrapped around my legs as I try to walk.

Courage in my Carry-On

The moment when a baby places her hands on my face and looks deeply into my eyes is special.

How am I so blessed to be in this place?

After playtime, it's dinner, bath time, worship time, and then bed.

We get on the bus at 6:30 pm to go back home.

It's been a month since I boarded the plane for Uganda and already time seems too short.

Eventually, my time here will come to an end, but the impact these little lives have on me will last long into the future.

I had travelled enough to know that the honeymoon stage of a new country can wear off, and then the culture shock and homesickness sets in.

This trip homesickness happened to me a few days before Christmas, my first ever Christmas away from my family. As usual, I was one of the quieter volunteers of the group. I had no problem connecting and loving the babies, but I struggled with connecting with the staff and nannies at the babies home. Once again, my insecurities were rearing their ugly head. I was so quiet, one of the nannies told me, that the others were asking if I could talk. I was upset, not by their words but from the feeling I was failing because I had come to Africa to make a difference.

Rachel Hamilton

I wrote in my Journal:

I felt God call me to this place, yet it feels like I am failing. How can I make a difference when no one sees me? How can I create change when I don't have a voice? Why was I given the dream if I am not useful? I am struggling alone. I want to change lives, but I feel locked inside myself. This road shouldn't be so rocky, why do I feel so numb, don't you hear my cry, God? I walked out of my comfort zone, yet this is my reward. Do I care too much? Am I trying too hard? Why do I feel like a shell? I am so overwhelmed by the need. Everywhere I look people need hope, need money, need someone who cares. God, please help me love your loved ones. I need your grace, and strength. Be with me, carry this weight.

It seemed to me that with every new culture it was two steps forward and three steps back in my personal growth. One volunteer I had grown close to was Chosen. Chosen was from Australia and she had been volunteering for a few months before I arrived. She is the type of person you only meet once in your lifetime. Kind, strong brave and leaves a lasting impact on everyone she meets. She was so kind to me and took me under her wing. With her love and support and those of the other volunteers, I slowly started opening up again.

Then after a few weeks in I fell in love and it was love at first sight. Deep down I knew he was the one. He

Courage in my Carry-On

was about six months old and he was sitting on a mat surround by the other babies who were laughing, crying or playing with toys. What struck me as beautiful was he was just sitting there quietly; gentleness and calmness seemed to surround him. He was the most handsome boy I have ever seen. That was it, I knew one day he would be my sponsored child.

Sponsoring a child means committing to sending money monthly to support the child and his or her family, the funds are used for a variety of benefits, healthcare, education, clothing, and more.

We worked hard, but my time in Uganda was not all diapers and feeding. The organisation also wanted volunteers to enjoy the tourist opportunities that Uganda offered. So, one weekend I and a few other volunteers headed to Jinja. Jinja is a very popular tourist destination because it's where the source of the Nile is. If you like adrenaline-packed activities, then it might just be the place for you.

We stayed at the Nile River Explorers camp located on the banks of the Nile river.

I decided to go Quad biking. It was a good choice for riding a bike at high speed along the dusty road was exhilarating. An added highlight was as we wound through small villages, the local children came running out shouting "Muzungu, Muzungu."

Rachel Hamilton

Muzungu means foreigner or white person, and I had grown used to hearing the word whenever I was out in public places. It was always said with such warmth that I never felt there was any negative connotation connected to it.

After two hours of bike riding, we were covered in red dirt. What better way to cool off than a swim in the river. Once we were dry again, it was on to the next activity of horse riding along the banks of the Nile river. I had ridden a horse many times but never along the banks of the Nile. Just like Angkor Wat, it was another 'pinch-me-am-I-awake?' moment.

We arrived back in Kampala refreshed and ready to start another week of volunteering.

I loved volunteering with all the different ages but the big toddlers were my favourite because they were able to talk and interact with me. It was funny how well behaved they were with their nannies but if I told them to do anything, they just laughed at me.

Another room I worked in was the nursery. The preemies and newborns were here. I loved it because it was very hands-on, including hourly bottle feeding, bathing and checking their vitals. It was humbling to care for these priceless lives.

Courage in my Carry-On

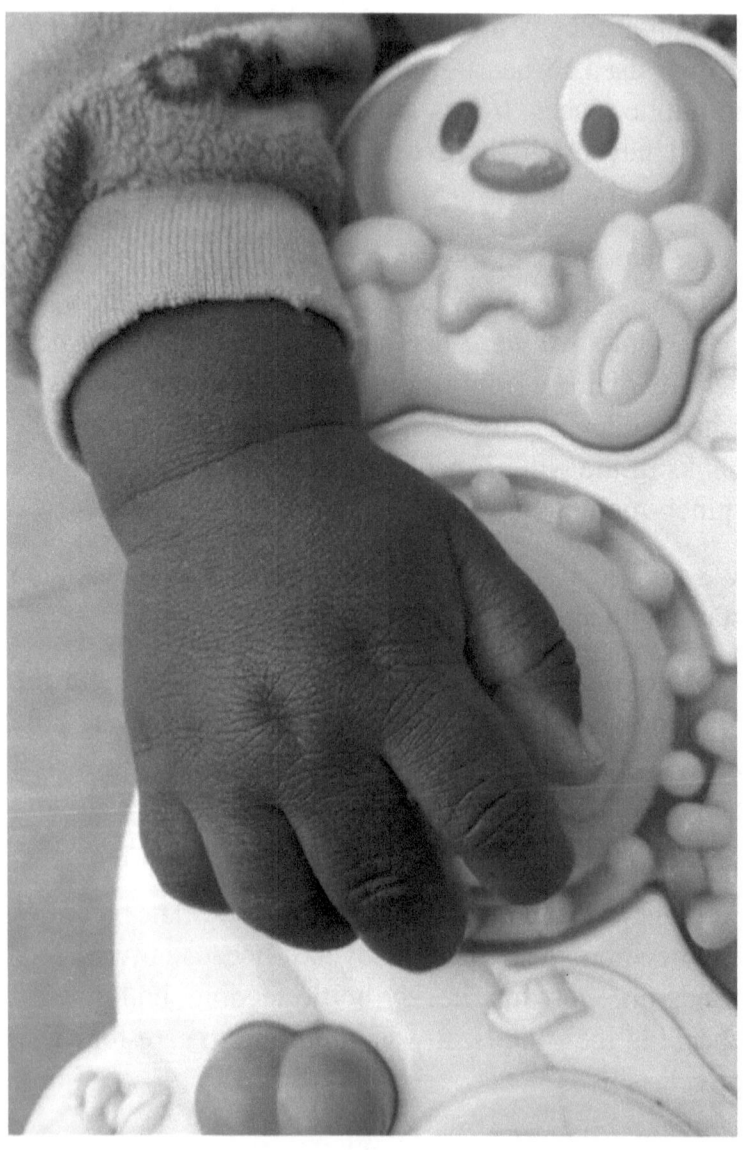

Spending time with the babies Uganda

Rachel Hamilton

Each month a volunteer meeting was held, this was a day when you would meet with the volunteer department staff, to get to know them better, have a nice meal and share what we were learning from our time of volunteering. It was also a time to connect with other volunteers who worked in other departments of the organisation. The highlight was a big cake to farewell all the volunteers who were leaving that month.

Often, we inspire one another in ways we are quite unaware of. Freddo inspired me as I watched him rushing around serving others and attending to the needs of the volunteers. One day in particular he was run off his feet. I could tell he was very tired but never once did I hear him complain, instead he smiled as he continued putting everyone at ease. Freddo probably doesn't even remember that day. But the way he selflessly served and gave 110% really impacted me. People like Freddo are the reason so many volunteers lives are changed, because he lives out his faith through his daily actions, care and support.

When I first came to Uganda, I had an idea that it would be this adrenaline-filled adventure where everything was new, strange and overwhelming. While I have had moments like that, I didn't realise how normal it would quickly become. Before long Uganda began to feel like home as the culture shock wore off.

The three months flew by and once again it was time to

Courage in my Carry-On

say goodbye and head home. Deep down I knew that Uganda was not finished for me and I would be back one day. Then suddenly I was back in Australia. But only for a few days as I was going to New Zealand for a couple of weeks to see friends and help my parents work on the family home.

Blog Post:

March 17, 2017,

4:30 am and in just half an hour I'm heading to the airport for the second time this week.

At this moment I'm thankful for jet lag which makes it easy to wake up early, it's also a reminder I will have been in three different countries in the last ten days.

It's a strange feeling not knowing where I call home anymore. It's almost like I am a child of three families. I have a birth country New Zealand, Australia is my place of residence and work, and Uganda is where I feel deeply alive, where every day is an opportunity to make a difference.

There is something about different countries and cultures that makes my heart sing. If money was no object, I would become a gipsy, and spend my whole life falling in love with cultures and countries.

It is hard coming back to reality.

Rachel Hamilton

I'm struggling with the lack of freedom we have here to make a difference.

Red tape, legal, and political correctness binds and hinders us from being able to get in and create change.

It frustrates me that you have to have a degree, do a short course, or wade through piles of paperwork to be able to do anything worthwhile.

Don't get me wrong, I know there is brokenness, needs and opportunities to make a difference here.

I'm not hating on the western culture.

But as someone who doesn't have any great wonderful talents or useful skills but passionately wants to make a difference in the world, I struggle in this culture of degrees and systems.

There is a reason I'm back home, a purpose for these frustrations, feelings and thoughts.

As each day goes by, I'm learning to live this new kind of normal.

I'm thankful to be a Kiwi living in Australia and the opportunities these beautiful countries provide me.

But I'm also thankful for this dissatisfaction, because it means Africa has grown and challenged me.

Courage in my Carry-On

Blog Post March 29th 2017.

It's two weeks since I arrived home and a painful reality has finally hit me; I'm no longer in Uganda. I've pushed these feelings away, with everything being a whirlwind of activity it's been easy, jet lag, three days in Australia then jumping on a plane and coming to New Zealand, scraping wallpaper, painting, falling into bed each evening so tired and achy from the physical work. I don't want to face these feelings or look back, but process them I must.

Uganda my third home, how I adore and love you, it's strange to think the first month I would have given anything to jump on a plane and fly home.

But as the days turned into weeks and weeks into months I began to adjust, adapt and see how Uganda has deeply impacted me. With each country I visit, it continues to amaze me that I arrive intending to change lives, but it is me who is changed by the time I go home.

Rachel Hamilton

Holding a snake at Entebbe Zoo Uganda

Each situation is an opportunity for growth, insight, healing, and restoration; not just in the lives around

Courage in my Carry-On

me but my life too.

The other trips I have been on, I have come back feeling broken by the injustice, sin, sorrow and sadness of the world. Broken by the things I have seen, like the woman in the red-light district, trapped in a life of slavery in Thailand, and the little boy who asked me to be his mother in the orphanage in Sri Lanka.

But this time something beautiful has happened, I have come back, healed, and filled with joy from seeing the things God is doing, and the knowledge that there IS something I can do to make a difference.

I've seen hope, in the laughing eyes of happy healthy babies who have been rescued, in the new school where hundreds of Children can now safely study all year-round.

Uganda has shown me I want to devote my life to something bigger than myself. I want to use what I have to make the world a better place and it's possible. We can do it.

Hurt is everywhere, need is everywhere, but we can be part of the change. I don't have to be in Uganda to make a difference, I just have to have open eyes, and hands ready and willing to help those around me.

All I want to do is get on a plane and go back, but for now, I will take the knowledge and lessons I've learnt, and aim to make a difference where I am right now.

But I will be back, dear Uganda. I will be back.

I was back in Australia in body but every day I was thinking about what the babies were doing. I imagined them playing, eating, and sleeping. Yes, I was obsessed, everything told me to go back to Uganda as soon as possible. I went back to my job and started saving as much money as I could. Every hour at work I was thinking how much closer I was to flying back to Africa.

Blog Post, August 1st 2017:

After three months of living in Africa my whole worldview, and even how I view myself has changed.

It is my life has restarted.

My emotional, physical and mental well-being are completely changed.

4 months on and in 4 days I board a plane to Uganda again.

I would have never imagined I could go back to the country I have grown to love so soon.

This time I plan to go back with a greater passion to serve. I aim to be worthy of the privilege of living in Africa for two more months.

Courage in my Carry-On

I am excited at the prospect of seeing the beautiful people I love, overjoyed to see the babies that stole my heart four months ago.

I pray that my heart is pure, and I act in a way that honours everyone I come in contact with

Rachel Hamilton

Back to Uganda

6th of August 2017:

I'm once again standing in Entebbe airport. Yahoo, I was back. Freddo was there to pick me up and it felt like coming home.

There were a new set of volunteers to get to know along with a few familiar faces.

Julie (from the USA) had been there on my last trip. Julie inspired me with her love of Uganda and doing her part to make a difference in the lives of everyone she interacted with. She welcomed me back so warmly that any threads of homesickness and apprehension disappeared.

I was told later that the staff were very surprised I came back. They thought I would be the last one to return

Courage in my Carry-On

because I was so reserved and quiet the first time I was there.

Blog Post, August 15th 2017:

I've been back in Uganda just over a week now. Such a joyful time. Days pass by in a happy blur; dishes, dirty nappies, cuddles, warm welcomes, baby laughs, bumpy bus rides.

Coming to Uganda for the second time has been everything I dreamed of and more.

My heart overflows.

I feel so loved, so welcome, and so wanted.

This time I didn't have the struggle of culture shock. Instead, it felt comfortable to walk along familiar streets and know where to go when I needed groceries.

I was beginning to gain confidence and become more open in my interactions and my heart overflowed to hug and kiss the babies and children. My future Sponsored Boy had grown much during the four months I had been away, and I was delighted to see how strong, healthy and healthy he was.

The weeks passed in a happy blur of activity. I wanted to do something touristy again and I thought no better way to cross something off my bucket list than to go white water rafting on the Nile river. So, Jane (from Australia) Alyssa (From Canada) and I headed to Jinja.

Rachel Hamilton

We had talked to other volunteers who had done it and they said it was great fun and I was excited.

When we arrived, there were a large number of tourists already gathered around the rafts. We were fitted with life jackets and helmets, and split into groups of six people per boat plus the guide. I happened to notice that our boat was all girls apart from the male guide, which turned out to be disastrous. We paddled along until we came to the first rapid which didn't seem that scary, honestly, I thought it was a bit boring. The sun shone down, and as we drifted along in the calm waters our guide suggested we swim for a bit. I slid into the delightfully tepid water and enjoyed swimming about. It was so relaxing. This was the life, I thought.

After a few minutes, we climbed back into the raft. Up ahead I could see white churning water.

"You must paddle to the right so we don't go into the grade six rapid," Our guide, Josh, warned us.

A grade six rapid is a long rapid with a strong undertow. My knuckles went white as I gripped my paddle and dug it into the water as hard as I could. As we slid into the white water, we paddled with all our might, but unfortunately, because we were a boat of females, we didn't have the strength to fight the current and we were sucked into the danger zone.

Then suddenly, the whole front of the raft was flung high

Courage in my Carry-On

into the air, flipping the raft and sending us crashing into the mercy of the undertow. White water engulfed me, muffling sounds, as I spun round and round. Everything moved in slow motion as my mouth filled with water, and my legs fought for survival. I thought of my family back home, and my life up to that point, had I done everything I was called to do in this life?

After an eternity I felt my life jacket pull me to the surface, but to my horror, I found I was trapped under something solid which turned out to be the side of the raft. I could hear Josh yelling that I was trapped. Then strong arms reached down and pulled me on top of the overturned raft, strangely I was still clutching tight to the paddle. Josh shouted;

"Hold on."

I wanted to, but as I looked around for something to grasp, another raft came crashing down on top of us and drove me down. Once again, I was under the white water, I couldn't breathe as I was trapped.

"I'm going to die," I thought.

A little voice in my head said:

"Time to give up fighting."

Then suddenly I was breathing pure sweet life-giving air, and I saw the welcome sight of a safety canoe. They grabbed me and took me to another raft. I felt weak as they pulled me up by my life jacket and I sat in silence. I was in such shock I couldn't utter one single word for ten minutes. I felt that I had come close to death. Had I? I don't know. The Nile river rafting has never lost anyone. Jane was as traumatised as I was and to this day we talk about how the experience has affected us, it forever bonded us together as close friends.

It gave me a reality check. Life is fragile, priceless, and the future isn't promised.

Am I living such a life, that if today was my last day, could I look back and say "I gave it all?"

Do I love enough, care enough, am I leaving footprints of good behind me?

Do I realise each day has a purpose and reason?

Life is a miracle and I must make it count.

1st of October 2017:

I flew back to Australia with the plan to save money and return to the country that makes my heart sing. Being home brought the all too familiar feelings that come with each re-entry.

Blog Post 4th of December 2017:

So overwhelmed. So many things I want to do. So

Courage in my Carry-On

many lives I want to change. Yet here I am, feeling a failure.

It's two months since I returned from my second trip to Uganda.

I'm letting people down, I know it and I'm not proud of it.

Over and over I'm reminded that an empty jug cannot fill a cup.

Yet I feel so distant from the only One who can fill me.

Struggling to be a good friend, to keep up with the simplest tasks, let alone deal with the important things pressing on my mind.

People don't talk about the cost. The price of following where God leads.

We just see the glory, the inspiration, the courage of great men and woman of faith.

We don't see their tears before and after their journeys of faith.

We don't see the valleys of doubt, fear, and loneliness that comes alongside the joys of following Christ.

The thing is, when you've been changed by steps of faith you can't go back.

I'm never going back to the one I was before I went to

Rachel Hamilton

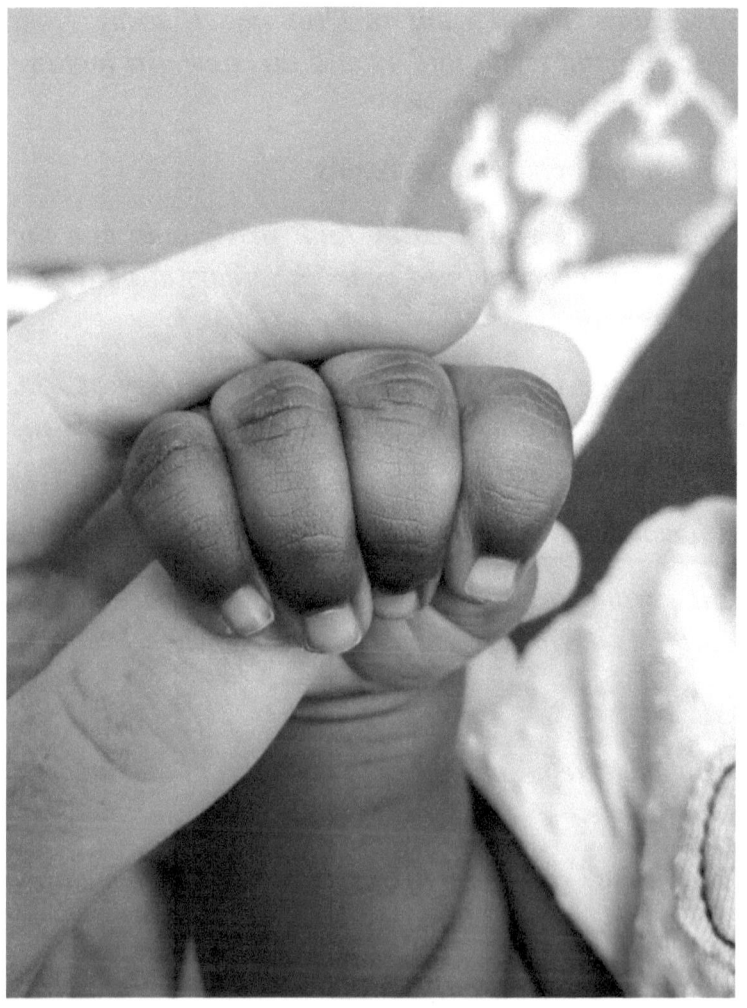

Tiny babies Uganda

Uganda and I don't want to.
But I've lost more than one friend.

Courage in my Carry-On

Some days I just want to shut myself away from everyone and try to understand this new girl looking back at me in the mirror.

I'm caught between two worlds.

I am the girl who lived by faith in Uganda and the girl who is overwhelmed by doubts, fears and failings back here.

Every time I step out in faith after every overseas trip, these feelings and struggles come to fight with me when I return.

Is it worth it?

Is it worth being so burdened down by the cares of this world? Is it worth feeling so lost at sea when I return?

100% yes.

With each step, I am closer to the heart of the one who died for me.

Every time I surrender to Christ's ways, I am becoming less of me, more of him.

In touching an orphan's hand, I touch the very heart of God because they are his children.

I will never be the same.

For the sake of his call, I will accept and embrace the cost.

Rachel Hamilton

Trusting that even when He feels so far away, God is holding me close, filling me with his love.

It was not long before I was feeling the pull to Africa strongly once again. Was it possible to go back a third time? My funds were low but thankfully the hotel where I worked became busy and I was able to pick up extra shifts, making the return to Uganda possible. By now packing was easy as I knew what I needed to take. As I excitedly filled my bag with baby clothes, the maternal feelings were overpowering. I held up the tiny cute outfits like an expectant mother and imagined holding the babies that would wear them. I was warm with love.

This time when I arrived in Uganda, instead of staying at the hotel in Kampala, they asked me to move into the volunteer accommodation at the Babies Home. This meant I didn't have to commute every day, I could just walk down the stairs and be with the children. It was so nice to spend more time with the babies and nannies. Most of the volunteers were living at the hotel, so for a couple of weeks, I was stayed alone. I didn't mind as it felt like home. Every night as I prepared for bed, I could hear muffled sounds of sleeping toddlers and the nannies who were working the night shift.

Each time I came to Uganda, my heart expanded more and more. I was falling deeply in love with the culture and adapting. I loved walking down to the roadside markets and buying fresh fruit and veggies; pineapples,

Courage in my Carry-On

passion-fruit, bananas, you name it. It was fun cooking eggplant dishes and baking homemade-bread. I was thankful Mum and Dad had unknowingly prepared me for this with my childhood in the country. I felt like I was finally becoming domesticated and I loved it. My relationship with the nannies was growing stronger by now. I was still quiet, but I was learning to share and open up.

Once again, the volunteers wanted to go to Jinja, and I decided to go again. This time they wanted to go zip-lining and bungee jumping. Zip-lining sounded fun, but I was not keen on bungee jumping after my experience with white water rafting. We drove into the jungle and climbed high into the trees. The view was incredible and it was great fun flying between each tree. Next, we headed to our accommodation on the banks of the Nile. Although I had been there before, it was a different view from the last two times, it was every bit as breathtaking, however.

After a night's sleep my teammates were ready to Bungee Jump. Before white water rafting, I would have done it no matter how scared I was, just to prove I was brave, but now, just watching them jump and hang by their feet made my stomach drop. I mentally rewrote my bucket list; less death-defying activities, more ice skating, and things that don't make my mum panic over my wellbeing.

Rachel Hamilton

After the break, it was back to days of babies smiles, first steps, and chasing toddlers. The moments turned to priceless memories. Then all too quickly it was over. I got back from Uganda in May 2018 a few days before my 27th birthday. Of course, I was planning my next trip, but my bank account was very unhealthy so I needed to work. My old job was there if I wanted to go back, but I wanted more job security than a casual job. I applied for over forty-five jobs but heard nothing and I was disheartened. For the first time in three years, Africa seemed out of reach.

One day I saw a job advertised for aircraft cleaners at the Sydney International airport. I was keen on it as it was a permanent-part-time job with five weeks of paid leave. This meant I could go back to Uganda for over a month and be paid the whole time I was there. I applied for it, but for three months I heard nothing, and my depleted bank account was dwindling. It was frustrating but at last I heard I had a job. When I finally had a starting date, I was jubilant, and once I started I valued every day of work because I had waited so long for it. The commute to and from work was three hours a day, with early morning starts (sometimes waking up at 2:30 am.) It was tough getting up that early but I didn't mind, all the hard-working people I had met through my travels gave me a new appreciation for honest hard work, and enabled me to embrace each new season (difficulties and all.)

Courage in my Carry-On

Working at an airport made the return to Uganda possible once more. Moreover, I loved working with people as passionate about travel as I was, and enjoyed talking with them.

One of my dear workmates, Kathy, gave me bags and bags of brand-new clothes, books, shoes and donations for the babies, when she heard of my plans to go to Uganda. I was overwhelmed by her generosity and kindness. The time flew by and before long I was packing my suitcase once again. The day before I was due to fly out, I put the last baby bib into my bag, sat on the lid and flicked the catches shut. I was ready.

5th of June 2019:

One day after my twenty-eight birthday I was on my way to Uganda for the fourth time. This time it was a well-worn path I was travelling. The distance between Africa and Australia seemed to be shrinking. It had been over a year since I had been there, the longest wait between my trips, and lots had changed, but once I arrived it felt like I had never left.

This time most of the volunteers lived at the Babies Home, so I was only at the hotel for one day before moving to the volunteer accommodation near the Babies Home. I was overjoyed to be reunited with the nannies and babies. My Sponsored Boy had moved into the village, and as I was his sponsor, I was allowed to visit him and his new mum and brothers. They greeted me warmly and I instantly fell in love with his family. He was so happy, healthy and well adjusted.

This trip I had the sense to savour every moment. Who knew if I would be able to come back for the fifth time? I savoured the red dirt between my toes, the skin-to-skin moments with a premature baby, the days spent with the big toddlers who ran to me when I entered the room, shouting:

"Aunty Rachel."

I loved these kids. I loved this culture.

Then it was over, the month had passed and I was heading back to Australia, full of memories, overflowing with love. As the distance between me and Uganda widened, I was struck with the knowledge that I was no longer fearful. I no longer questioned if I was good enough or if I had importance. I knew deep down I was worthy, my travels had taught me that fitting in isn't the end goal, and this was just the beginning of becoming beautifully, unashamedly me.

Courage in my Carry-On

Heroes

Boarding a plane back in 2011 may have been the first step that started change in my life, but the real heroes of my story are the irreplaceable people I've met in the last ten years, who have touched, challenged and shaped me into the person I am today.

Brian, Peace, and Hope, who worked behind the scenes are three of these people. They helped me get to Africa and always made me feel valued and welcome. I am forever changed by their love and acceptance, and appreciate how they gently encouraged me to become more confident as a volunteer.

Jasmine from the USA (who volunteered with me during my second time in Uganda) moved to Australia for a year in 2019. She stayed with me and my family for the first few weeks after she arrived. We had fun together and she cheerfully put up with me when crazy things happened (like the time I lost the car in the airport parking lot when I went to pick her up.)

Then there are Esther and Jane, who live near me in Australia, and are always sending me messages of support and encouragement. I feel strengthened when we reminisce over shared memories of Uganda.

Carks Isaac who I met in Uganda has become the third little brother I have always wanted. He forever changed the way I view myself and how I interact with the world. His unconditional love and acceptance of me opened my heart, and taught me that people may be born into different cultures, but deep down we are all the same. We love the same, hurt the same, feel the same.

The young newly engaged couple Brenda and Syrill who run an orphanage and school in a slum, are another inspirational couple. Day after day they work hard and selflessly give everything to feed, clothe and educate children.

Then there are all the other amazing people I met on my trips; from my fellow volunteers, team leaders, staff, pastors, nannies and caretakers, in fact, every single person who is in my life right now. These people have taken the time to talk to me about their courageous life journeys. They are the unseen ones who every day make choices to bring hope and healing to the world.

Courage in my Carry-On

This is my message to everyone who wants to make a positive change in a hurting world:

You are a world changer. You are touching and impacting many lives even though you don't realise it. Your weakness and even your failures are all part of a bigger picture of hope. You are changing someone's world by your faithfulness, courage and compassion. Just keep taking small steps to your dreams and see what happens. Thank you for being you.

Rachel Hamilton

Your Story

I may not know you personally, but I want you to know that you can be brave just like me.

Do you feel misunderstood?

Do you feel that you don't quite fit in?

You matter, oh you matter so much. Your story isn't finished.

Darling, you will say the wrong thing sometimes, and that's OK. There will always be someone more talented than you, and braver than you, but no one can ever be you. You can never be replaced. Don't lose heart.

I see you. How amazing you are.

Maybe somewhere along the way, someone told you a lie and you believed it.

Courage in my Carry-On

You were told that you lacked worth and value; you were handed a poisoned apple of self-hate and you ate it core and all.

I feel your pain like it was my own, see the thin mask you wear, trying to act so strong but alone in a dark room, crying yourself to sleep.

How I wish I could reach you, wash your fragile heart with the truth.

The truth that you are valued, unique, wonderful, important.

Set apart, seen, loved, cherished.

I pray for you, believing one day you will know the truth.

Self-hate is a loud and mean bully, self-hate tells you to compare yourself to those around you.

As you have read, I was unbelievably shy, I wasn't adventurous, and I struggled to communicate. I couldn't connect with people on a deep level because I was afraid to show the real me. I went through most of my teen years feeling disconnected. I felt broken inside,

But this journey of self-discovery has taught me that I am ok just the way I am, and every life matters, including mine.

Like me, you need to embrace the fact that you were

created to scatter light, and designed to change lives. As you step outside your comfort zones and feel the freedom of being unashamedly you, you will be empowered to use your uniqueness to touch lives.

I love genuine people who are comfortable with their own crazy. And daily I am falling deeper in love with my own crazy.

Some people are not going to get you, but darling trust me, someone is praying for someone like you.

The older I get, the more I am embracing the things that make me, me.

We don't have to justify who we are to anyone.

God has made you to stand out and shine, and darling you do it so well.

Keep shining, your uniqueness is wonderful.

Please don't believe the lies that you have to change to be loved, wanted, and chosen.

You are a valuable one-off work of art.

I've learnt that small actions create big change over time and the greatest thing in the world is love. Radical, unconditional love.

To create change, we must become love. This means we need to rise above petty arguments and disagreements.

Courage in my Carry-On

To be grateful for everything. We are not always going to have the same convictions, but as we learn to respect and encourage those around us.

Maybe you have gone through something painfully life-changing. Something that shook your whole world. Greatness is not easy. Greatness is not born from fairy-tale endings. Pain creates endurance.

Pain is a price many are not willing to pay. If you have pain you have a gift. Not a gift you ever wanted but a gift, nevertheless, because you do not have a choice in carrying this torch. You did not have a choice to bypass this journey. You must walk this path towards the end goal of greatness.

You have a higher purpose. I don't care what limitations you face.

They do not define or restrict you.

Sometimes life will feel like a summer storm.

Recently I have been tried by personal storms, sickness, stress, and the loss of a friend to cancer. These difficulties have left me feeling empty. I'm like a broken jug, who wants to fill those around me, but the life-giving water keeps running out.

Yes, people around us walk through things more terrible than we could imagine, but it doesn't mean our smaller pain doesn't count.

Rachel Hamilton

Your pain matters, your storm is real, your courage is visible.

Let's be kind to ourselves and hold tight to the knowledge that summer storms don't last forever.

At the time of writing this book, the world is in the middle of the Corona Virus pandemic. Who knows what international travel will look like on the other side of this crisis? Fortunately, a step of courage does not have to begin by going on a plane (this is just my example of becoming brave.)

Your life journey may be completely different. Your first step might be opening up to someone and asking for help, or making small changes every day to do something that is challenging for you. Whatever that first step may be, tuck courage in your carry on and take that first step.

Courage in my Carry-On

Thanks

Thanks, ZealAus Publishing for your hard work and professionalism throughout the publishing process.

Special thanks to all my Logos Hope shipmates who were there at the very beginning of my journey. Sarah and Vinzent, Rachel, Dana, Sue Lee, Andrew, Ian, Adam, Aronu, Bapi, Giribabu, Bubuna, Grace, Grace Lee, Lydia, Sony, Sinoj, Wico, Samuel, Jijo, Helen, Alfred and Helen, Lawrence, Evangeline, Saravanan Yoshi, Peter, Joanne, Agnes, Patrica, Kerry-Ann, David, Enn Jung, Agnes, Natasha, Lia, Antia, Grace, Lydia, Lucy, Danree, Jimmy, Hyeji, Anna, Simon-Peter and Anna, Sol, Jessica, Lita, Kathleen, Alex, Alexis, Bradley, Emma, Eunha, Hema, Judith, Kanako, Katie, Nathalie, Paola, Rachelle, Yanina, Esther and loving memory of Megan.

Rachel Hamilton

Thanks to my dear friends during my Cambodia and Thailand trip.

Lynda, Jack, Jake, Pam and Warwick, Dyvia, Danielle, Emily, Landon, and Alana.

To the Staff that helped me get to Uganda Ebony, Adrienne,

Ebony, Adrienne, Freddo, Peace, Brian, Hope, Ruth, Shirley, KerryAnn

First trip to Uganda

Volunteers Melody, Jill, Stella, Vanessa, Catherine, Stephen, Sarah, Julie, Solvie, Maria, Mariah, Aly, Sarah-Moon, Megumi, Joanna, Jamie, Jessica, Lynn, Elisabeth, Laura, Debby, Marcel, Thomas, Victoria, Gabrielle, Lise, Yonne, Georgia,

Second trip to Uganda

Jasmine, Jane, Esther, Kayleigh, Jane, Arielle, Jess, Julia, Kelsie, Heidi, Rachel,

Kirsty, Hannah, Jamie, Janicke, Jesssica, Alisha, Viktor, Vanessa, Heather,

Courage in my Carry-On

Third trip

Samantha, Krista, Karl and Kaylee, Lisanne, Samantha, Sarah, Pleun, Ludo,

Fourth Trip

Lukas, Karissa, Mikylla, Rachelle, Brittany, Bryanna, Courtney, Paula, Rachel, Krista, Azia, Loraine, Loren, Caitlin, Rumbidzo,

Staff at Babies Home.

Doreen, Jonita, Steallah, Genavive, Maria, Truth, Sarah, Immaculate, Alice, Allan, Faith, Brendah, Christine, Patricia, Bella, Emma, Salome, Ruth, John. Phiona, Getrude, Margie,

Rachel Hamilton

About the Author

Rachel Hamilton loves traveling and volunteering. When she's not catching a flight or planning her next adventure, she can be found spending time with her family.
Find her on Instagram @rachhamy

Other Books By ZealAus Publishing

Wendy Hamilton

Eating a Light Bulb does not make you Bright
Light on Home-schooling
I told you not to Climb the Cactus.
Surviving the Badlands of Motherhood
Darling the Window is on Fire
Love and House Renovations in New Zealand
Homemade Church

Surviving Home-Schooling Through the Corona Crisis

Shipwrecks and Bush Felling

Children's Novels

Little House in the Bush

The Britwhistles win a Prize

The Britwhistles and the Elasticizer

Rachel Hamilton

Children's Picture books

The Unlucky Snails

The Unlucky Snails go to France

Ruth Hamilton

Children's Picture books

Lilly Gets Left Out

A Very Good Wife Is Hard to Find

The Candle Tree

Boris Bottle the Late Bloomer

Susie Solves the Case

Diana and Her Crocodiles

Henry and the Hot-Air Balloon

Courage in my Carry-On

Rachel Hamilton

<u>Batalhas Ocultas: Pureza, Deus, Rapazes e Vida</u>

is the Portuguese translation of

Hidden Struggles: Purity, God, Guys and Life

Janine Williams

<u>Homesteading Rescue Remedy</u>

Host WWOOFers, Create Income, and Restore Order to Your Overgrown Acres.

These can be found at

www.zealauspublishing.com

www.ingramcontent.com/pod-product-compliance
Lightning Source LLC
Chambersburg PA
CBHW021155080526
44588CB00008B/343